visions of myanmar

text and photography by
James Muecke

*Dedicated to the friendly, enthusiastic and devoted team of eye surgeons
at the Yangon and Mandalay Eye Hospitals*

acknowledgements

My sincere thanks and appreciation must go to a number of people who have helped in the production of this book. Dr Henry Newland and the Department of Ophthalmology at Royal Adelaide Hospital have provided the platform and the funding to make my trips to Myanmar a possibility. Liesl Ross from Medical Art & Design and Alan Hoare from Clinical Photography at Royal Adelaide Hospital have worked tirelessly to help create a colourful and enduring record of modern Myanmar from my rolls of slide film, and their respective Departments have contributed generously towards the process. My wife Mena, has been a wonderful help and support throughout, from the selection of photographs to the layout of the final images, and my parents, Peter and Jan, have helped with a number of excellent editing suggestions.

Thank you also to Peter Fisher who imparted a number of invaluable photographic and post production tips and generously lent me one of his superb cameras for my final trip this year; to Caroline Webber who guided me through the complex printing process; and to Dr Thant Thaw Kaung in Yangon who has been of tremendous assistance in facilitating and arranging distribution of my book in Myanmar.

My colleagues in the Department of Ophthalmology have all given their time voluntarily and have happily shared their knowledge and skills during our numerous trips to Myanmar. I greatly appreciate their dedication and efforts which have ensured the continued success of the Vision Myanmar programme.

I would also like to make a special thank you to the generous contributions of Pfizer Ophthalmics, AMO Australia, Allergan Australia and Novartis Ophthalmics who have helped to fund the production costs of my book.

Published by James Muecke, Department of Ophthalmology, Royal Adelaide Hospital

Copyright © 2005 James Muecke

First published August 2005

Text and photography by James Muecke

Photograph selection and layout by James and Mena Muecke

Graphic design and pre-press by Liesl Ross, www.medicalart.com.au

Image enhancement and colour management by Andy Purgacz 0421 618 564

Printed by SNP Leefung, China, www.snpcorp.com

ISBN 0-9756093-0-0

All photographs have been taken using a Canon EOS SLR camera with Fuji slide film. The images have not been digitally altered.

introduction

The images presented in this book are a selection of those taken during the four trips I have made to Myanmar as part of an ophthalmic surgical team from Royal Adelaide Hospital in Australia. The two week trips were divided between the Eye Hospitals in Yangon and Mandalay, where we consulted and operated together with the Myanmar eye surgeons. The weekends were free and gave me the opportunity to explore a little of this vast and mysterious country – a land of extraordinary colour and beauty with a warm, friendly and gentle people.

The hundreds of ancient temples at Bagan are an overwhelming spectacle and one of the true wonders of South East Asia. The towering Shwedagon Pagoda and the mighty golden boulder at Kyaiktiyo are mesmerising in their splendour and tranquillity. The bustling streets and markets of Yangon and Mandalay, the banks of the majestic Ayeyarwady River, the rickety teak marvel of U Bein's Bridge and the serene fishing villages of the Rakhine Coast provide an ever-changing feast of colour, activity and intrigue. It is certainly the most captivating country I have ever visited – a photographer's dream and a traveller's paradise.

The thought of compiling a book of photographs only arose when I was cataloguing the slides from my second trip. I was so thrilled with the results that I felt compelled to share the beauty and fascination of Myanmar with the world. I also found that the light for photography in Myanmar is at its best in the early morning and late afternoon. The colours are greatly sharpened and enriched at these times, bringing life to subjects which may appear washed out in the full light of day. So on my subsequent trips, I rose before sunrise each morning to prowl through the streets and villages and returned before sunset each day to catch Myanmar at its best.

Ultimately, photographs can only satisfy our visual appetite. It is impossible for my images to convey the experiences that bathe the other senses as one travels through Myanmar – the myriad of food aromas that burst from the street markets, the gentle chanting of Buddhist monks at the pagodas, the warm blanket of humidity that envelops you during the day or the calming breeze that accompanies first light – for these and many other extraordinary experiences, you will need to travel to Myanmar. Hopefully I have inspired you!

James Muecke

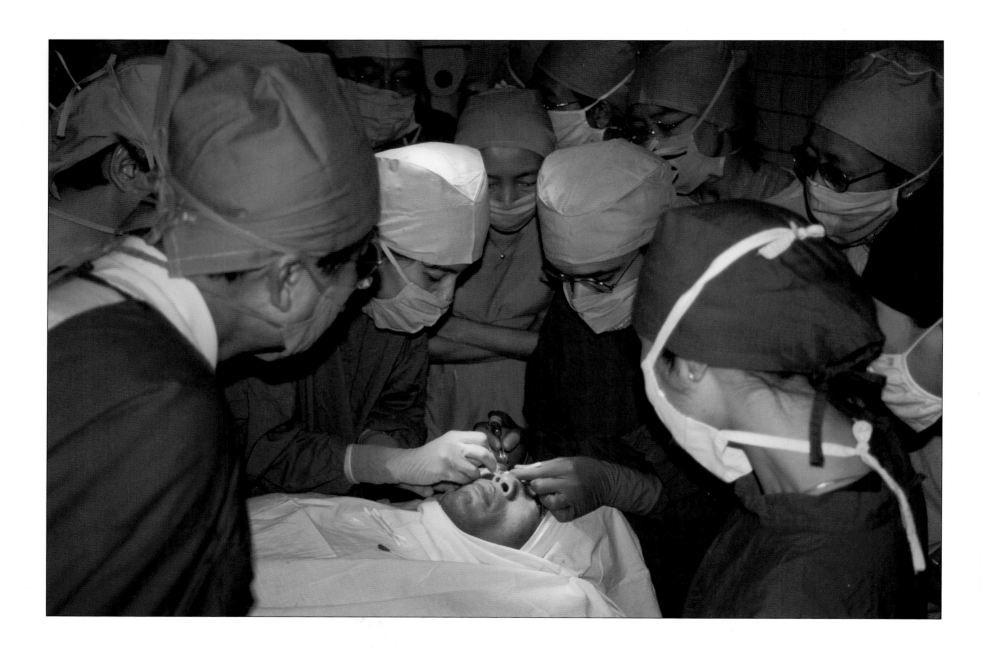

vision myanmar

The "Vision Myanmar" programme was first established in the year 2000. It is a collaboration between the Departments of Ophthalmology at Royal Adelaide Hospital in South Australia and Yangon Eye Hospital in Myanmar. The aim of the programme is to enhance the training of eye surgeons from Myanmar and Australia and ultimately to enhance the eye care of patients in both countries.

Consultant eye surgeons from Royal Adelaide Hospital travel to Myanmar for a two week period every year. During their intensive days reviewing and operating on patients with significant eye diseases, the Australian team share their knowledge of current ophthalmic diagnostic and management techniques with the Myanmar eye surgeons. The Australian doctors benefit greatly from their time in Myanmar, inevitably being presented with a multitude of challenging eye problems and having to operate on a concentration of cases that they would only be exposed to over a year or more in Australia.

Much can be achieved during the short visits, but the most successful way to teach an eye surgeon is to offer extended "fellowship" training in subspecialty areas of the profession. Royal Adelaide Hospital has already trained one eye surgeon from Myanmar in advanced retinal surgery. Dr Mya Aung is the only ophthalmologist in a country of fifty million people capable of performing advanced retinal surgery and is now passing on his skills to his own "fellows" at Yangon Eye Hospital. We are currently training a further retinal surgeon as this book goes to print and will be training fellows in other subspecialty fields of ophthalmology in the years to come. Plans are in place for trainee eye surgeons from Australia to spend time as fellows at Yangon Eye Hospital, learning forms of surgery to which they have little exposure back home.

Vision Myanmar goes further than this, with close collaboration on clinical research projects and public eye health programmes. Currently, the eye surgeons from both countries are working together to raise the awareness amongst the people of Myanmar of the blinding complications of diabetes on the eye, an ever-increasing problem in developing urban centres all over the world.

The Australian eye surgical team give their time and knowledge voluntarily, however funding is a constant necessity to help sponsor the trips and to cover the costs of public eye health projects. All profits from the sale of this book will be returned to the Vision Myanmar programme and will benefit the eye health of countless people.

Left – Dr Dinesh Selva (at the head of the patient) from Royal Adelaide Hospital shares his surgical skills with an enthusiastic group of ophthalmologists at Yangon Eye Hospital.

Right – Dr Garry Davis from Royal Adelaide Hospital examines a patient with ophthalmologists at the Mandalay Eye Hospital.

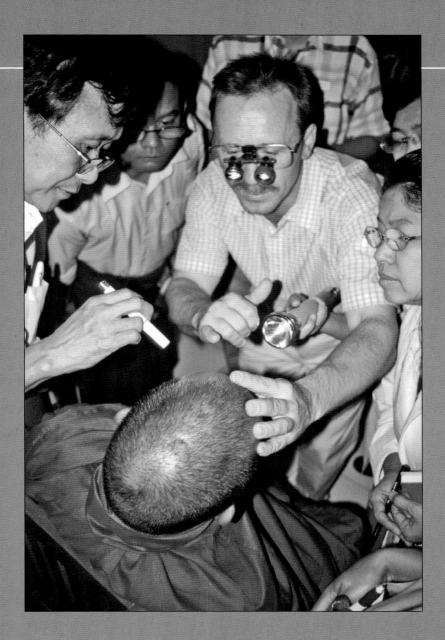

myanmar

Myanmar achieved independence from a century of British rule in the years following World War Two. In 1989, the English name Burma was changed back to Myanmar, the official name of the country for at least five hundred years before the British arrived. Myanmar now refers to the entire country and does not identify the nation with any particular ethnic group.

Many of the geographic names which had been in place since the British Period were also changed, so as to bring the pronunciation closer to that of the original Myanmar names. The capital Rangoon became Yangon, the ancient city of Pagan became Bagan, the sea port of Sandoway became Thandwe and the Irrawaddy River became the Ayeyarwady River. The hill station of Maymyo, re-named after a British officer, Colonel May, once again became Pyin U Lwin. The name Mandalay has not been changed.

contents

yangon

Page 12 (previous page)
Panoramic view of Old Yangon with the Yangon River beyond.

Pages 14 to 19 – The Shwedagon Pagoda
The extraordinary golden stupa of Shwedagon Pagoda or *Paya* was first erected at least 1000 years ago. It has been destroyed by earthquakes on numerous occasions and the current form dates from the mid 1700s.

Above left
A team of craftsmen meticulously replace the gold leaf cladding of the Shwedagon, a task that must be repeated every four years.

Below left
The central pagoda is surrounded on all four sides by a multitude of shrines, temples, stupas and pavilions.

Right
An intricate web of bamboo shrouds the entire Shwedagon Paya and offers protection for the craftsmen working beneath.

Pages 16 and 17 (previous pages)
Shwedagon Paya is Myanmar's holiest shrine, and all Buddhists in the country hope to pray there at least once in their lifetime.

Left
Hundreds of oil lamps surround the base of the Shwedagon and form an elaborate offering to Buddha.

Right
The Shwedagon soars nearly one hundred metres from the top of Singuttara Hill in Dagon Township.

Above left
The stately India House in Ahlone Township of Yangon.

Below left
Sule Paya in Central Yangon, said to be over 2000 years old, is used as a milestone from which all locations in the country are measured.

Right
The Archbishop of Yangon's House behind St. Mary's Cathedral in Botataung Township.

Left
A man surveys the frantic scenes in the street below from his second story balcony.

Right
Elelgant shuttered colonial houses line the narrow streets of Old Yangon.

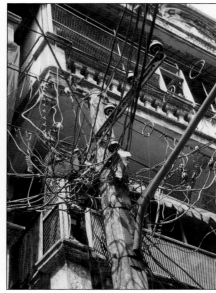

Left (clockwise from above left)
Young men toil around the clock to load and unload the multitude of cargo boats that line the busy riverside wharves at Yangon; a woodworker carves religious figures in a small workshop on Gyatawya Road below Shwedagon Paya; chaotic electricity wiring in the streets of Old Yangon; one of the many street-front hardware stalls in the "Iron Bazaar" district of downtown Yangon.

Right
Laundry hanging in shuttered upper story windows is a common sight through the narrow streets of Old Yangon.

Above left
A trishaw owner haggles for business.

Below left
Men playing checkers on the pavement in Old Yangon.

Right
A heavily loaded bus making its way along Strand Road.

Left (clockwise from above left)
Brightly coloured flowers for sale on a sidewalk in Central Yangon; one of the many street markets that line much of the free space along the pavements of downtown Yangon; roadside food stalls abound in Central Yangon and become very active at dusk when hungry workers finish for the day; a hawker prepares a betel nut chew or *kun yar* on his mobile stand.

Right
A mother and daughter shopping at the market.

Page 34 (overleaf)
Merchants and customers alike start their day before first light at Thirimingala Market.

Page 35 (overleaf)
Stalls and vendors selling mouthwatering fruit and vegetables line the entrance to Thirimingala Market.

Left
Fried local delicacies for sale on the sidewalks of Old Yangon.

Right
A makeshift tea shop on the sidewalk of Sule Paya Road in Central Yangon. Tea shops are an important part of life in Myanmar and offer a relaxing opportunity to catch up with friends and colleagues.

Above left
A man delivers a load of woven plastic bags suspended from a *hta po* balanced on his shoulder.

Below left
A barber dozes whilst waiting for business in his street-front shop in Central Yangon.

Above right
A trishaw loaded up with empty wooden crates leaves the market.

Right
Large blocks of ice being delivered by trishaw.

kyaiktiyo

Page 40 *(previous page)*
Dawn at Kyaiktiyo. Kyaiktiyo is the second most sacred Buddhist pilgrimage site in Myanmar after Shwedagon Paya in Yangon.

Above left
A bullock cart loaded with hay plies the road near the town of Kyaikto.

Below left
Low tide along the river at Kyaikto.

Right
Women picking flowers in a field near Kyaikto.

mandalay

Page 54 (previous page)
The imposing walls of Mandalay Fort in the early hours before sunrise.

Above left
One of the main crenellated gateways into Mandalay Fort. The Fort was built by King Mindon in the mid 1800s and protects the Royal Palace which lies deep within its long walls.

Below left
The old Clock Tower, erected in honour of Queen Victoria, stands proudly at a busy intersection in Central Mandalay.

Right
Bicycles are a very popular mode of transport in Mandalay.

Left
Mandalay is an important religious centre and boasts many fine Buddhist temples, pagodas and monasteries such as Sandamani Paya (above) and Kuthodaw Paya (below).

Right
Young novice monks hitch a free ride on the roof of a minivan. Every boy in Myanmar is expected to become a novice monk or *samanera* for at least a few months before the age of 20.

Above left
Novice monks line up with their black lacquer bowls for daily alms-giving. Providing food to the monks attains merit for the donor and enhances their karma or *kan*.

Below left
Myanmar nuns, or *thilashin*, must shave their heads and wear pink robes.

Right
Unlike monks, nuns collect dry food provisions or money only every week or two.

Page 62 (overleaf)
Charming pre-war vintage buses still ply the dusty streets of Mandalay.

Page 63 (overleaf)
Large banners with bright slogans are a common site in Mandalay.

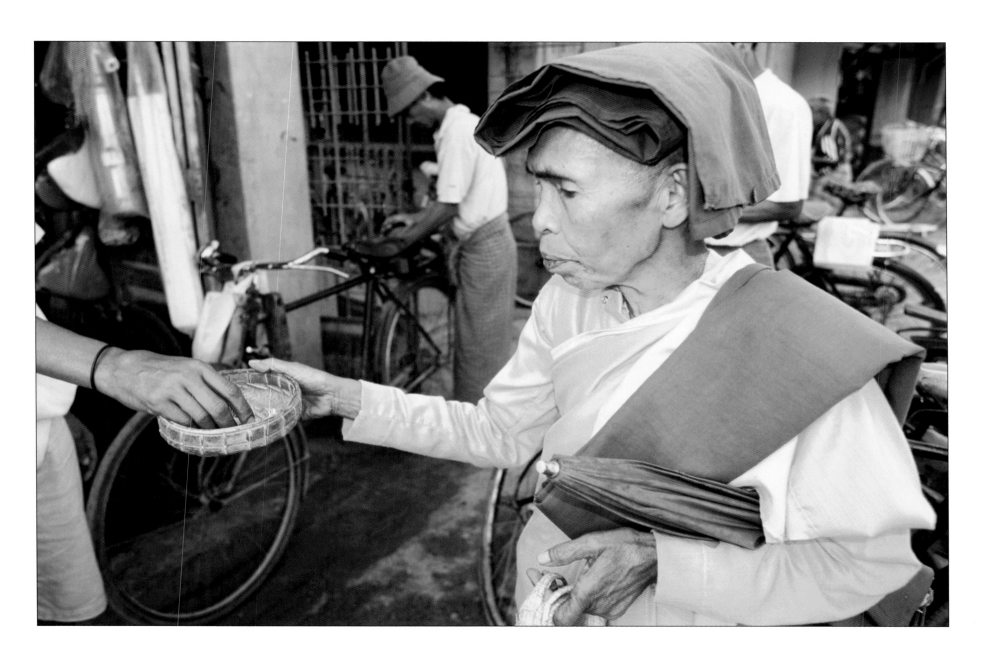

★ Oppose those relying on external elements
★ Oppose those trying to jeopardize stab
★ Oppose foreign nations interfering in interna
★ Crush all internal and external destructive

People's Des

Page 64 and 65 (previous pages)
An appetising selection of local produce for sale at the Kaingdan Market. The sellers take great pride in arranging their fare in an attractive and enticing manner.

Left
A typical colonial era house in Central Mandalay.

Right
A young girl working with a road construction team takes a break during the intense midday heat.

Above left
Young boys playing in the sand along the banks of the Ayeyarwady River in Mandalay.

Below left
Young men playing cane ball or *Chinlon*, a skilful blend of soccer and volleyball.

Right
The squatter villages along the banks of the Ayeyarwady in Mandalay are a source of constant activity and fascination.

Above left
A woman washing the family's clothing in the river water.

Below left
Colourful sarongs or *longyis* drying on a raft of logs moored to the river's edge.

Right
A young girl wearing traditional makeup or 'thanaka' to protect her skin from the fierce sun. Thanaka, which also has a cooling effect and astringent properties, is applied in a unique and decorative fashion by females and young boys throughout Myanmar.

Left
Goods being unloaded from a barge along the Mandalay riverfront.

Right
A pile of terracotta pots awaits delivery at the edge of the river.

Left and right
The impressive ruins of Mingun Paya in the ancient city of Mingun, just upriver from Mandalay. The pagoda was never completed and was subsequently destroyed by an earthquake in 1838. What remains is a massive pile of bricks over 50 metres high. If completed, the pagoda would have been the largest in the world, soaring to over 150 metres in height.

Above left
A raft of logs rests at Mingun on its long journey down the Ayeyarwady River.

Below left
Ferries and barges moored along the riverfront at Mandalay.

Right
A traditional house in the village at Mingun.

Above left
The grand Candacraig Hotel at the former British hill station of Pyin U Lwin in the foothills of the Shan Plateau.

Below left
Pyin U Lwin, or Maymyo as it was called in the British era, is located in the highlands above Mandalay. It is blessed with a wonderful collection of Tudor style colonial mansions, where the British came to escape the stifling heat of Upper Burma. Myanmar gained independence from Britain in 1947.

Right
Colourful horse-drawn carriages are still a popular form of transport in Pyin U Lwin.

u bein's bridge

Page 80 (previous page)
U Bein's Bridge near Mandalay just before sunset. The bridge was built nearly 200 years ago using teak pillars taken from the abandoned palace at nearby Inwa.

Above left
Monks strolling across U Bein's Bridge near the former capital of Amarapura.

Below left
U Bein's Bridge is the longest teak span bridge in the world, stretching more than one kilometre over the shallow Taungthaman Lake.

Right
Tourist sampans with their colourful prows, moored on the edge of Taungthaman Lake.

Left
A monk dressed in exquisite orange robes walks across U Bein's Bridge to Maha Ganayon Monastery.

Right
Ice cream for sale at one of the many sheltered rest stops along the Bridge.

Left and right
Late afternoon scenes at the magical U Bein's Bridge.

Above left
Women fishing in Taungthaman Lake near U Bein's Bridge.

Below left and right
Serene images of Taungthaman Lake around U Bein's Bridge.

Left
U Bein's bridge is a constant source of fascination and wonder.

Right
A lone cyclist returning home to his village across U Bein's bridge.

bagan

Page 92 (previous page)
A hot air balloon takes off for a dawn flight over the archaeological wonder of Bagan. This awe-inspiring ancient site covers an area of forty square kilometeres along the eastern bank of the Ayeyarwady River in central Myanmar.

Above left
The elegant Htilominlo Pahto, is one of over two thousand temples, shrines and stupas built over the dry dusty plains of Bagan during the 11th to the 13th Centuries.

Below left
The massive unfinished Dhammayangyi Pahto, is the largest temple in Bagan. Built in the late 12th Century by King Narathu, it is an example of the 'hollow' style of temple, or *pahto*, which typically contain a variety of Buddha images.

Right
Mingalazedi, built in the late 13th Century by King Narathihapati, is an example of a solid stupa or *zedi*, which are said to contain relics from the Buddha.

Left
The brilliant golden sikhara of Ananda Pahto towers to over 50 metres. The whitewashed temple was built in the early 12th Century by King Kyanzittha and is one of the finest and most revered in Bagan.

Right
Gawdawpalin Pahto, built in the early 13th Century, was badly damaged by an earthquake in 1975. Following restoration, its *sikhara* now soars to a height of 55 metres.

Left and right
Detail of the superb stone carvings and bas-reliefs that decorate the exterior of Bagan's temples and stupas.

Above left
Young novices at the beautiful carved teak Nat Taung Monastery on the edge of the Ayeyarwady River.

Below left
The rest house or *Zayat* of Taung Bib Monastery acts as a meeting place for pilgrims during religious festivals.

Right
A cloud of dust rises from a lone horse-drawn cart as it navigates the network of tracks that weave between Bagan's ruins.

inle lake

inle lake

Page 108 *(previous page)*
Sunrise over the tranquil waters of Inle Lake in Shan State.

Above left
Stilted bamboo huts hover over the 'floating' islands of Inle Lake. The man-made islands are created by the lake dwelling people, or *Intha*, who draw together masses of soil and vegetation and peg them to the shallow bottom with bamboo stakes.

Below left
The islands provide a highly fertile base for the widespread cultivation of fruit, vegetables and flowers which are then sold at the daily markets.

Right
Intha fishermen use these large conical nets to fish the shallow waters of Inle lake.

Above left
The larger villages, dotted around the lake, are dissected by narrow canals lined with stilted teak houses, shops and handicraft factories. Each village has its own 'specialty', such as woven silk, parasols, silverwork, ironware, pottery and cheroots. The popular mode of transport through the narrow hyacinth-lined waterways are flat-bottomed canoes propelled by oars or paddles.

Below left
The 'floating' villages support a number of beautiful wooden monasteries, highlighting the importance of Inle Lake as a religious centre. Nga Phe Monastery is famous for its performing cats, who have been trained to leap high in to the air by the resident monks.

Right
A unique 'hanging garden' suspended beneath the eaves of a house.

Above left
A couple of villagers enjoy a quiet cheroot while catching up on the latest news.

Below left
A group of young boys eagerly await repairs to their kite.

Right
A lone boatsman demonstrates the traditional leg-rowing technique typical of Inle Lake.

Above left
A silk weaving factory in the village of Inn Paw Khone on the south-western edge of the lake.

Below left
Dyed silks drying in the sun.

Right
A silk weaver working at her loom.

Left
A village elder enjoys a quiet cheroot.

Right
Nam Pan village is famous for its *cheroots*, the traditional hand-rolled cigars which are enjoyed throughout the country.

Above left
Lake-dwelling Intha people arrive at the market in Nam Pan before sunrise. The "five-day markets" are held every morning at a different village around the lake.

Below left and right
Cartloads of bamboo for sale at the market.

Left and right
Wafers, dried noodles and nibbles for sale at the Nam Pan market.

Left and right
Young boys learning the trade at the morning market.

Left
A spectacular "long neck" woman of the Padaung tribe, from the mountainous Kayah State south-east of Inle Lake, has travelled to the region to make and sell her traditional woven fabric. A single brass ring is added each year from the age of six, gradually depressing the collarbones of Padaung women and making their necks appear more and more stretched.

Right
Brightly coloured woven shoulder bags for sale at the Indein market.

Page 134 and 135 (overleaf)
Sun-dried chillis, *zee tee* (a type of plum) and maize are just some of the exotic foodstuffs available at Inle Lake's markets.

Above left
A teak bridge crosses the canal from Indein to the Nyaung Ohak Monastery.

Below left
The covered stairway leading to Shwe Inn Thein Pagoda, overlooking the village of Indein. The roof of the walkway is supported by hundreds of carved teak columns and is fringed by a multitude of vendors selling handicrafts, antiques and religious artefacts.

Right
The hill above Indein is studded with an extraordinary forest of crumbling stupas that radiate out from either side of the covered stairway.

ngapali beach

Page 138 (previous page)
The sun sets on another glorious day at Ngapali Beach. Located in Rakhine State in western Myanmar, Ngapali Beach overlooks the Bay of Bengal south of Bangladesh.

Above left
A boat unloads its cargo onto waiting bullock carts.

Below left
A fisherman casts his net into the shallows of Ngapali Beach.

Right
Tiny crabs create a myriad of spectacular designs in the moist sand, as they tirelessly re-empty their burrows following the tidal retreat each day.

Above left
Fresh water is carried to the boats of fishermen preparing for their long night on the open waters off Ngapali Beach.

Below left and right
Fishing boats depart each day at sunset, and the daily cycle of Rakhine coastal life continues as it has for centuries.

mrauk u

Page 156 (previous page)
The imposing Htukkan Temple, built in the late 16th Century, is reminiscent of military bunker but was most likely an ordination hall or *Thein*. Inside, a maze of dimly lit passageways, lined with hundreds of Buddha images and bas-reliefs, penetrates toward the inner sanctum.

The eclectic collection of pagodas and temples which make up the archaeological site of Mrauk U date from a powerful dynasty established by King Minzawmun in the early 15th Century. The glory of this dynasty was brought to an abrupt end following annexation of the area by the British in the late 18th Century.

Above left
The fortress-like Kothaung Temple, built in the mid 16th Century, stands sentinel over the surrounding farmland.

Below left
The village of Mrauk U sprawls haphazardly amongst the crumbling pagodas and ruins of the old palace and city walls. The village lies at the source of Aungdat Chaung, a tributary of the great Kaladan River in the very north of Rakhine State in western Myanmar.

Right
Hundreds of carved stone stupas adorn the tiered exterior of Kothaung Temple.

Left
Ornate Buddha niches punctuate the layered octagonal base of one of Mrauk U's graceful stupas.

Right
Serene Buddha images, such as the famous statue in Thatkya Manaung Pagoda ordination hall, grace many of Mrauk U's holy sites.

Left
A passenger obligingly walks alongside his trishaw as the driver pushes the cycle up a steep hill.

Right
A team of bullock carts ply the parched fields on their way to work.

Left and right
Village life in Mrauk U has changed little over the centuries.

Left
Water collection is a never-ending chore for the women and children of Mrauk U.

Right
Children enjoy a refreshing shower from one of the many wells that water the village.

Left
The women transport water from the wells or creeks using silver vessels characteristically nestled on their hips or balanced on their heads.

Right
A man waters his field of flowers with an ingenious irrigation device made from rusty tin cans.

Left
Small creeks or *chaung* dissect the village, acting as playgrounds for the children and a convenient means of transport for the villagers.

Right
Wooden boats and sampans ply the Rakhine waterways, propelled by sails sewn from lengths of bright plastic or colourful patches of cloth.

Left
Rafts of bamboo are slowly punted along the Laymyo River to markets downstream. The lengths of bamboo are hewn from the great forests that swaddle the hills of the Chin State, to the north-east of Mrauk U.

Right
Facial tattooing is unique amongst females of the Chin tribe, a form of adornment celebrating their passage into womanhood. It is said that their faces were tattooed in order to dissuade the unwelcome attention of men from neighbouring tribes. Girls are no longer tattooed, using thanaka as a convenient, temporary and painless substitute.

Left
Low tide along the banks of the murky Kaladan River. The Kaladan is an impressive stretch of water that begins its journey among the gentle mountains of the Chin State to the north and empties into the Bay of Bengal at the former colonial port town of Sittwe. The five hour journey upstream to Mrauk U must be taken by wooden boat from Sittwe.

Right
Fishermen enjoying the tranquility of the Kaladan River at dawn.

Page 176 (overleaf)
Golden haystacks, like mammoth mushrooms, litter the fields of Rakhine State and supply sustenance to livestock through the long dry season.